Blundstones and a Brown Dog

Also by Christopher Nailer and published by Ginninderra Press
Peel Street

Christopher Nailer

Blundstones and a Brown Dog

Acknowledgements

Several of these poems have appeared in *Quadrant* and one in *The Best Australian Poems 2005*, edited by Les Murray (Black Inc.)

Special thanks to Paul Miller for the cover image.

For Claire, Helen, Kate, Lindsay and Ruth

Blundstones and a Brown Dog
ISBN 978 1 74027 392 3
Copyright © text Christopher Nailer 2006
Copyright © cover image Paul Miller 2006

First published 2006
Reprinted 2015

GINNINDERRA PRESS
PO Box 3461 Port Adelaide 5015
www.ginninderrapress.com.au

Contents

Monday's busker	7
Army photographs	8
Cold Canberra mornings	9
Local library	10
Konfrontasi in Melbourne	11
Frost	12
Core samples	13
Sunshine and flowers	14
Commune in the bush	15
The hurry	16
A Message from the Chairman	17
A fencepost for Lizette	18
Rehearsal space	19
Aristophanes in Greek	20
Coming of age	21
Conversation with the teeth	22
Transit of Venus	23
HR	24
Singapore weekend	25
The heart chamber	26
Hieroglyphs	27
For Pam going hiking in the Pyrenees	28
Anniversaries 2005	29
Backing singer	31
Bali wind-chime	32
Blank verse	33
Business trip	34
A death on the campus	35
Fly screen	36
Grey travellers	37
Life after death	38

Mango	39
Mortuary Station	40
Mother-daughter	41
Midnight bus…	42
The man on the 38 bus	43
New steam age	44
On the underground	45
Packing for Ruth	46
Fair Celia	47
Pink balloon	48
Rationing	49
Shaft of light	50
Skateboard king	51
Snail armadas	52
Specter Gang, Shinjuku	53
Videoconference	54
Wishing and imagination…	55
Jazz hands	56
Cub nights	57
From no place and to every destination…	58
Diseases of the heart	59
Fridge door	60
Life class	61
Friday night in Mandalay	62
One starry night…	63
Perspective	64
Armistice in Brunswick Street	65
Sabina's violin	66
This is the bed…	67
The toymaker	69
Song for Anna's third wedding	70
Ode to an antique typewriter	71

Monday's busker

Monday's busker's learning how –
empty streets, slim pickings, but the acoustics
off the cement go well for practising

Tuesday's busker gets small silver –
it's pensioner-night at the cinema and there's
not much spare

Wednesday's busker plays for secret lovers –
a quiet restaurant pretends to be a business meeting;
they don't listen

Thursday's busker plays for the sick,
the old, the unemployed –
a dollar from the dole cheque is not too much

Friday's busker's an egotist –
plays loudly and off-key at the heaving crowd;
not giving, swearing – a feeling shared

Saturday's busker's professional –
every amateur is out
but there's good money for the best

Now Sunday's busker offers to the god of showmen;
and perhaps if the markets are kind
they'll give him Monday off.

Army photographs

Faces keen and dutiful, light and merry,
steady and soldierly, smooth, scruffy,
snapped at the end of training,
or saluting the colours on the King's birthday,
or the day of embarkation –
There's my father, second back row,
third from the right – looks like
there'd been some celebrating the night before.
And there's one or two others my mother remembers –
she danced with this one; that one bought her drinks;
the fellow there took her flying in a Tiger Moth
and was warned off…
The rest are nameless.
Who knows what you thought or who you loved?
whether you drove like a madman or
played the fool or had a good singing voice
or were kind to the girl you married?
And did you make it through?
And were you happy?

Cold Canberra mornings

Cold Canberra mornings give away
who studied where and when;
the China scholar in padded Mao jacket
is all grey now;
the Japan student warms arthritic hands
over a thermos of green tea;
the Indonesianist,
a talismanic scrap of batik underneath,
wears whatever he can get;

And at the bus stop, vetting grants to education,
a middle-aged Melbournian
pulls a Magpies beanie tight over his ears,
hooligan-like;

Those wanting mystery hide their affiliations;
a black woollen overcoat is good
or a shapeless heavy jumper
or a jacket with a hood,
or they brand themselves alternate –
bright waterproofs, couch bicycles,
or briskly pace through parklands –
Blundstones and a brown dog –
looking neither right nor left.

Local library

You wouldn't think to find it here
but there it is, on the bottom shelf:
Bishop's *Studies in Chinese Literature*
with Hightower's famous paper on
'The *fu* of T'ao Ch'ien.'
Thirty years ago a young man
sent away for this on microfilm;
And bingo! some eccentric's left it
to the local library where,
looking for a casual read one day,
I bumped slap into this old friend
with a remote and troubled past
and grasped him warmly by both covers.

Konfrontasi in Melbourne

In dead of night with a crystal set,
earthed through the fly-screen
down to an ice-pick, buried deep
among the parsley and the silver-beet,
aerial tacked into a cement crack
high up where the wall of the sleep-out
met the four-inch planking of the veranda roof –
Frank Ifield in the earpiece and Connie Francis –
flick flick –
Migrant station:
syncopations,
jagged instruments,
the news in Greek:
bla bla Flemington bla bla bla
Mr Menzies bla bla U-Thant bla bla bla
Tunku Abdul Rahman.

Frost

Night's cold breath
lays down filaments,
etching the open spaces
with a crisp rime,
sparing only shadows –
the night's antithesis

Slant sunrise delights
a hundred billion spectrums;
fresh footsteps crunch
the fog's white cities;
the dog's warm nose
makes rivers run.

Core samples

At 30,000 feet the faeces separate;
it's the change in pressure, the dehydration,
the tension before landing;

That yellow layer's the dahl from Mughal's in Delhi;
the red's the pasta sauce from Zeffirelli's in New York;
that dark bullety layer's the roast pork from
Dragon-Phoenix in Shanghai;
that's why the hotel gym is so important –

Executives relive their meetings in the lavatory,
each stopover ruled off with a moist crease,
clear as the expense report. It seems
even the bowel's got a view on globalisation.

Sunshine and flowers

She had the longest brown legs
and her smile brought summer;
I dreamed of her constantly,
everything, silently...

shy of her beauty;
she treated me sisterly;
I fell into hell.

And suddenly
nothing was like her smile each week
down the long hospital corridors –
its sunshine and flowers.

Commune in the bush

Great trees exhale
their mist onto the
corrugated iron roof;
it trickles at night
into the water tank
put in before the fourth wall
when the cash ran out.
The bush watches
this three-sided box
and all the human comedy.

It was cold those winter nights.
The mother and the baby
slept by the iron stove;
frost called on the raw plank-ends
of the unfinished room
where the two men slept.
And in the morning
you'd turn the one brass tap
and like magic there'd be
just enough to brew a kettle
for the two men, one woman
and the baby's milk.

The hurry

Two big men in a tiny car,
like cartoon elephants from a children's picture book;
It bulges round them fit to burst, tyres hard to the bitumen.
Where are they going so fast and
with no hint of a smile?

A Message from the Chairman

(50th Anniversary of the People's Republic of China, 1 October 1999)

A father walks his boy over the long week's holiday,
looking in the showroom windows,
waiting, hoping.

That day the radio cracked and hissed and that voice
made the hairs on people's necks stand up...

Same clips repeat in twenty colour sets:
Japanese invading over the Wall, bombing Shanghai,
the Chairman looking out from Tiananmen,

state visits, oversized armchairs,
Mao, Deng, Jiang impersonating statuary;
even the Americans –
Nixon, Carter, Bush – look monumental;
brows of the interpreters frown history in between...

The man tips a coin down the slot-machine;
Sprite thumps in the outlet guaranteed to fizz;
the little boy skips.

So we didn't go to war;
families still have children;
80% believe the next decade will be better;
middle-class is close enough to touch it, smell it:

What happened to 'Serve the people?'

Take heart, old fellow, here's two certainties:
You've got to get him dinner before sundown;
he'll want a toy fighter jet tomorrow.

A fencepost for Lizette

The trouble with living in the bush
is people dropping in –
those tyre-tracks never meant to be
a circular driveway –
she needed a post to fence it in.
So one hot summer I dug a hole as deep as my arm,
spaded and scrabbled out the clay and pebbles,
city hands blistering, sun hot on my neck,
her mob visiting somewhere else.
Deeper and deeper,
digging down and prising out,
sweat drops barely softening the iron hard ground –
It took an outsider to do what had been talked about
over tea and rollies every night for weeks –
this was my rent and board.
And when the post was in, clay and shale packed
tightly round its waist, it stood there,
an accusing finger where callers used to drive in –
Someone knocked it flat the first dark night.

Rehearsal space

Somewhere cheap –
an old warehouse or
decommissioned factory,
someone's aunt's holiday place
by the sea, somewhere with
lots of space for shouting and
falling down, where imagined
walls, rocks, precipices unblock
the relationships of things;
perhaps a clapped-out piano for the lyrics;
a bunch of smaller rooms for
the one one-on-ones,
for stretching out against a wall,
watching sunbeams in the break, or
practising the repertoire with a look.

Needs to be near a pub,
cheap eating-places –
Lebanese, Chinese, Italian, Greek –
open all hours for the sub-plots,
the dark nights of alleyways
where life gets
the fire hose treatment,
all the rough justice needed
to hold the tension of one
unspeakably tender silence…
To temper bodies
in irredeemable conjunction with rhyme,
character, movement, plot, till nothing –
not even the holy soundings of the real stage –
shake them free.

Aristophanes in Greek

One word, one word,
glossary close by,
the curtain inches back
from blur to puzzle till
click
a door half opens;
a sense, contingent, shy, uncertain,
like a bee approaching a paper flower –
something not quite right…

Check the scent of grammar –
noun or participle, middle or passive?

Then the humour burns out
bold and brassy:
the idiocy of the rich,
the credulity of the simple,
the blindness of the pompous,
as clear and true depiction of the passengers
on any city bus as of the citizens of Athens –
two thousands years of parody in
one human lexicon.

Coming of age

Remember when a haircut meant
the continental barber with the
foot-pump chair and just two prices:
men and boys?
Remember the star-cut photos showing
neater versions of the young Elvis
or Johnny O'Keefe – a bit of a wave
tumbled forward just a little
and the sides brushed back,
glossy highlights and two-tone lapels?
On High Street between school and the tram
you always had to say 'Keep the front a bit longer'
as the scissors snickered on the black nylon comb.

And the first day you paid the higher price?
Change of pace:
a sharp dab of shaving cream on one temple,
a swipe round the ear and neck to the other,
and the horn-backed blade flipped inside-out
and the thwack thwack thwack of the leather strop
and the zit zit around the sideburns
and the score score score down the neck
then the quick dab of a hot towel and a
pffft pffft of scented water…
Eight bob and out the door to a
brisk cool tingling behind the ears
and just the hint of a swagger.

Conversation with the teeth

Plastic arch and barbed imitation ivory,
parts of his broken mouth
disinfecting in a glass the morning after;
a perfect fit for the artist's palate,
so ugly he would have laughed
but the sky was full of tears.

What for now?
No more stories for you,
no more pipe-stem or red wine…

Come, I'll wrap you in something soft,
tender for the words you touched,
in a white handkerchief for he
never was without one,
in a brown paper bag for a humble
faceless exit from the house

and into the final paradox labelled
'Rigid Plastics'.

Go and chew landfill.

My father's dead.

Transit of Venus

So she walked across his face
and continued on
and millions would have watched
except the clouds were threatening;

Her body made him blink,
her smile ambiguous,
her demeanour said 'impress me',
but the touch was wrong.

Almanac and calculus predicted it.

And every time he thought perhaps
the heat and light might overcome momentum
he got surprised:
Not this time.
Barely a shortened footstep and no hint of
retrogression, she moved on.

No royal fireworks, just the inevitability of
shadows falling elsewhere.

But the sun comes out –
and the maths is reassuring:
if not in eight then
every hundred and twenty years.

HR

Here comes the HR lady so calm and rational –
summertime, we're back into restructuring…

It's like a visit from a hospital priest:
beyond redemption?

Large offices, small minds, peas in a whistle

Ideas break like dogs in the surf, wild with joy;
Rip up this conversation; today perhaps she'll smile.

Singapore weekend

Saturday in a sarong
sharpening Lindsay's pencils –
flakes of wood and pigment
curl off the penknife blade and flip –
like highly coloured insects
some into, some outside, the rubbish-bin.
She prattles about things at school –
Beth's my best friend she's from England
and Edward's crazy and David makes weird faces
and this book's so fun and so is Mr O'Connell
he stole Mrs Middleton's blackboard ruler
and he pretends he's going down into the cellar to find it
and look what the cat's doing –
(inside-out, upside-down,
asleep in the middle of the chip-marble floor)
This is what it's for.

The heart chamber

Approach the heart chamber in fear and dread;
here lie love's flowerbed and winding sheet,
wallpaper from the birthing room, fresh armpit smells,
childhoods denying the rules of evidence –
the old king's view on guilt.

Don't look for answers, love passes through;
carry the unlived granite to glowing hearth.
Warmth catches anew. It is the ark's brief covenant,
the priest's transgression, the desert's cloak, the book
of every smuggled dreaming;

It is the seat of courage hears the breathing;
and even when its world contracts
to a small black ache and traps off to the cold north
and bleakest hibernation, tears swell, soften and
ready its blind walls for another touch.

Hieroglyphs

Here's a line of brave feet – a woman's –
concentrated, moving fast,
almost running, a fullness in the instep,
something sensual in the way the toes grip and release
leaving perturbations in the sand;
she's looking for something…

Here's a self-made man taking exercise in runners,
walking squarely, footprint like a signet ring,
he's missing what the woman doesn't say…

And here's a third set out of balance,
one toe kicks in, one toe digs out, one heel deeper
one heel lighter – an inconclusive battle
with the sand dunes in the sensible afternoon □
It's all a matter of inheritance, he says,
in his seaweed calling.

For Pam going hiking in the Pyrenees

Don't send us a postcard.
I don't want to see saccharin images
of snow-capped peaks,
whitewashed villages with terracotta roofs
or cheery gap-toothed yokels from Molvania.
I don't want to hear the dates and places or
where you lost your sunglasses or
how you bargained for the cottage crafts that'll
find their way into your suitcase uninvited.
I want to hear what it said to you –
a gradient of new questions.
Send us a photo taken by someone you love
scrambling up the steepest part of the track;
I want to see you rugged up, red cheeks,
hair in a mess, snow on your boots,
with a big fat grin.
Oh, and the horizon must be crooked.

Anniversaries 2005

For Neil Bowler

I am so tired of anniversaries;
it's 90 since Gallipoli,
60 since Hitler, Hiroshima, the Bomb,
30 since tanks rolled down the palace gates in Saigon

And already it's…

4 since 9-11 and
3 since Bali
> *Neil's crooked smile, stitches in his forehead on*
> *Monday mornings after rugby;*

and 2 since the Marriott Jakarta
> *I had a haircut there once;*
> *Jim and Ikuko had a close shave;*

and one since Madrid and just one since

> all the fair-haired kids of Beslan were going into class;

And all the papers stuffed with supplements…

And no doubt next year we'll remember
in Saturday Specials

> 56 dead in London and
> an Aussie pilot downed near Basra and
> countless dead Americans around Baghdad
> and another Bali

And maybe someone will manufacture

God knows how many million candles
for all the Jews and Afghans and Chechens and Palestinians
and Kurds and Iraqis and Sudanese…

How many more bloody anniversaries?

Backing singer

Out of the spotlight
at the back of the stage
near the drum kit,
a voice true as blue sky
lightens jaded lyrics.

The guitarist wakes up,
counterpoints her
cold shoulders;
anyone can do solo;
she's worth accompanying.

Bali wind-chime

They let it in through Quarantine
dam bamboo din

She hung it on the clothesline
dong billabong

And as she did the towels and shirts and underclothing
bib biddy girdle ditty daddy bottle dilly dog

the women of the village walked beside her in the twilight
fragrant flowers in their hair.

Blank verse

Piano keys mostly and cricketers in the distance
and the picket fence round the field;
flag-poles, paint cracked and peeling in the sun;
rocks round the cenotaph and the soldier
at the heart of every country town.
Translucent parts of eggs and the corners of an eye
(don't shoot until you see the...)
milk bottles on the doorstep in the old days.
Chef's puffy self-raising hat and the waiter's napkin;
ice cream, whipped cream and the froth on cappuccino.
Flyaway hair of a favourite honorary aunt.
Christening smock, first communion brides,
nurses' headcloths and taut, fresh hospital bed linen;
Anglicised surname of a cheerful Viennese Jew;
chalk on the headmaster's cuff,
sail on the horizon,
a government position paper,
shirt-front of the family dog
and talcum on your lover's shoulder.
As a sheet, as a ghost, and a long hard party night.
Something bottled for covering up mistakes, hence also:
Chinese funeral gown, snow in Afghanistan,
seagull poo on the railings at the beach and
the spotless gaiters of the marine brass band.

Business trip

I used to leave with such alacrity,
the bag half packed,
just fresh shirts, socks, underpants,
shaving kit to add,
then to step out, keyed up,
for the cab ride to the airport,
skies beckoning
and the flush of indispensability
in another town.
Now I dread it, mope about,
can't decide which trousers,
overcoat or none, what book to take…
the dog sniffs at the dusty suitcase;
Helen says, 'Don't buy expensive perfume,
just come home…'
My grounded feet go slowly
down the cattle race
like any hundred others.

A death on the campus

The crow's corpse was already coming apart;
a halo of flies was busy at it,
rats, maybe a roaming cat had gone to work
and the warm sun sweetened it

just where I take a short cut
round the Screen & Sound Archive;
my foot shied and my stomach afterwards,
almost stepping on it in the long spring grass.

And each day, and for two more weeks
it was still there, its gown no longer glossy,
its arms no longer raised in speculation,
no defence even for its null hypothesis;

Finally the ride-on mower came by,
chopped up the big bits, spat out the small bits
leaving a random scattergram of primary evidence:
every scholar's nightmare.

Fly screen

Fingers pried the mesh away;
it needs redoing. Nothing for it but
to buy new stuff, wedge the battens off,
relay it, tack it down,
scrape flaked paint off the old beading and
pin it back with brads.
Some apprehension: this was *my* old handiwork:
Will the tacks come out?
Will the wood come off straight?
The old man frowns over my shoulder as I
set to with hammer, trusty old buggered-up chisel…
And sure enough, the strips ease off, and look!
the old blue-cut tacks haven't even rusted;
'Run 'em through your hair first' he always said.

Grey travellers

For Alex Whitworth

Travel companies have read all the demographics
and so, instead of bikinis, the posters now have
fit retired couples barefoot on the beach,
footprints that ebbing waters soften,
muted skies, greyish, twilighting,
quietly paced as the crabs come out of hiding.
Night fishers fill oil tanks in the boat harbour,
light their lamps, adjust bilge cocks, loosen their tackle.

But it's these same rocks we stumbled over,
this salt that made the wounds smart,
this sand we measured the years by,
these dumb gulls we threw the chips at that the children left,
cliff-tops where we dreamed great dreams upon the stars…
And out there a tough old sailor rounds Cape Horn
in a ten-metre yacht. Bugger tranquillity.
The sound of big waves crashing; that will take us out.

Life after death

The body begins to rot
from the flesh around the toenails;
dead cells glued up with soap
and talcum and renegade sock fibres
accumulate in that crevice where
man-horn erupts;
Here they build their brave new world –
a thriving, all-consuming
everlasting cosmopolitan cheese of
life after death.

Mango

Man is drawn to this fruit;
its comforting shape,
pregnant with potential fits, just so,
into the curve of his hand,
sweet scent rising in the sun
from pores where the juice swells
and splits the skin, dense, syrupy,
emerging bead-like, pungent;
The fruit draws him with its coyness,
halfway between firm and hesitant;
his job is to approach, alert to
any sign the ripeness is pretended,
but persistently; it's a coaxing but
with undeniable momentum;
Something says 'yes, it is time to eat',
and something else says, 'yes,
what took you so long?'

Mortuary Station

They built the Mortuary Station
for continuous requiems,
great big arches each end
to let the trains through,
huge openings down the sides
to load the bodies, let the smoke out,
one priest of each denomination
on the platforms for the cargo,
big black engine belching
hellfire and damnation.
They sent off so many corpses
in the Great 'Flu it seemed
the whole world migrated,
stitched into salvation.

Mother-daughter

Cloning must be like this:
two women come into the café,
one older, one younger,
both tall, with elegant long faces,
the same arched nose,
the same grey eyes slightly hooded,
voices crisp, authoritative;
and in the same 'don't mess me about' tone
one orders tandoori salad,
the other, a cheese sandwich;
And the first raises an eyebrow…
You see, the clone –
no matter how you reckon it –
never totally catches up.

Midnight bus…

Midnight bus
rumbles through empty
on yesterday's yawns

lighthouse squares
lend dead shops
a flash of purpose

bench seats all tensed up
like a hospital waiting room
brave tomorrow's pain.

The man on the 38 bus

The man on the 38 bus
wears a beige felt hat;
the smooth texture,
the flawless curvature,
the subtle indentations,
like a fuzzy photo of a distant planet;

His ears stick out,
red moons on either side;
His neck makes pink auroras through
soft grey stubble;

The scrap of brim, a curt equator,
divides a northern hemisphere of hat from
all that is non-hat.

Does he sleep in it?
Does it sit on his table at night
like a magic pudding?
Does he have smaller ones to
warm his boiled eggs?

He sits motionless, two seats from the front,
day after day, solitary, out of place;

Mr Trilby –
a hint of birdsong once upon a time…

New steam age

Stainless steel machine
transports the creative class in Xintiandi;

Stephen Sun at the handle,
twist, knock,
shovels black grit into the basket,
locks tight, opens steam cock…

Lifts warm China cup,
balances it,
black oil dripping into a small white sump;

Ready with the steel jug,
opens the valve again, tweaking,
hissing through a milk of cows;

Pours then spoons
the perfect ratio for
a cappu-Chino,
gathering momentum now…

Shanghai morning's murder without the
Orient Espresso.

On the underground

Don't look at the person
in front of you,
next to you,
behind you,
especially if their gaze is
fixed on you;
don't question,
don't challenge;
don't move suddenly
or nod or wink
and especially
don't smile;
don't make any human sign.
This carriage goes express
to paranoia.
Breathe quietly.
The god of innocents
called in sick today.

Packing for Ruth

Fold this special piece into
fine linen; let it not jar edges
with the other pots;
interweave the brittle and the soft,
lay them offset, peaceful in the
cardboard box.
Take newsprint, carefully crunch
crash-mats for porcelain –
things to be unshocked –
take scissors, tape, close thoroughly,
describe with marker
and in words confess:
fragile is this life; let it not slip.

Fair Celia

He was something in palaeontology,
domed head, kind smile –
our families went blackberrying once
though we all knew he wasn't a real doctor.

He and his clipped rose English wife
lived not far; their daughter Celia
had fair hair, alabaster skin,
sat two seats away on the bus;

and I would puzzle the arithmetic:
how long could she stay nineteen?

And before I knew it good friends were
doctors of this and doctors of that –
linguistics, history, maths, economics…
They couldn't cure anyone either.

And suddenly here I am, working on hypotheses
and propositions and models and proofs…

and my daughter yells,
'Hey, absent-minded professor, anyone home?'

One cold day long ago in faraway England
Fair Celia put her head into an oven
and not all the learned papers in the world
could bring her back.

Pink balloon

Pink balloon,
joy spent in climbing to the heavens,
in drifting over treetops, roofs, the lake,
till tired from the festive day
it fell in a car park sometime on Sunday night.
And in the morning the council man
with his long mechanical claw –
to save from bending for the plastic bags,
beer cans, cardboard coffee cups –
can't quite close his jaws round its
residual exuberance.

Rationing

They lived in a cottage
in a village owned by a Lord;
a low stone fence kept it
back from a postcard street.
In a small allotment
my grandfather kept chickens
and an old Ford with an
outside dicky-seat.
By the kitchen door was
a wooden water butt;
my sister and I could just reach
to float bits of wood in it like boats;
And on the threshold on one
of the few sunny mornings,
my grandmother urgently:
'You've got butter on
as thick as the toast!'
still raw from rationing.

Shaft of light

Shaft of light plays
through a window frame,
falls on fair hair, bodice,
one knee, a casually opened book,
leads a merry dance across a
deep burgundy oriental rug
to a door left questionably open;
Shaft of light's a Rupert Bunny smile
that puts a dagger through the heart.

Skateboard king

ka-lak d'orrrrrr klak
wheeled flight
a footpad streetcar named despair
d'orrr des' ka den
klak d'orrr klak klak
I am legion in my waist-tied anarak
klak klak
in every city at every ramp or step
d'orrr d'orrr
unheard king of the concrete armature
klak d'orrr klak
Unskilled?
Fuck
d'orr d'orrr d'orrrr d'orrrrr … … ka-lak!
Try that
Mr Centrelink

Snail armadas

After the rain great snail armadas
sail for worlds across the lane

to magazines of beet and squash
and golden dew.

My Gulliver-foot must pause mid-step
or crush like Drake.

Was Cortes really stout or just
a bastard in big boots?

My gastropods take Darien in
one long slow gentle slither.

Specter Gang, Shinjuku

The 'Specter Gang' had rocker hair,
short legs over big Hondas, Kawasakis, Suzukis,
red-lining every morning up the entrance ramp to Yamate-
dōri, deafening the pigeon-toed old ladies who step down to
the shops
in their modest plum kimono and white-mouse-like feet
and the bowed old men with walking sticks and bottle-end
glasses
who came home after the firestorm.
Night time the lads tumble out of red-lantern doorways
flushed, scrambling, slurring in junior-high English at the
foreign girl who steps off the 11.00 p.m. train from
Nihombashi
after coaching businessmen on
singulars and plurals.

Videoconference

The voice is firm, the words clear, the logic taut
and a quilt of tiny coloured tiles shows
a man not old not young whose
ideas roll as surely as the satellite;

Storms a hemisphere away then paralyse him;

Now multi-armed,

       his phrases more in hope than

              out of drowning;

Shiva disembodies his

       '…long-term strategic policy parameters…'

We watch his life disintegrate before us, till
finally closing, freeze-frame, a tile at a time;
one hand still raised in puzzlement –
She didn't call?

Wishing and imagination...

Wishing and imagination would
overfill the most expanding universe;
it's the vital anti-matter;

it's mass times desire...

Ask the janitor who sings arias in the basement;
his baritone rises from the same deep reservoir
that wants everyone to fly.

Jazz hands

Jazz hands, big and bad
cut chords thick as cockroaches,
bone hard was his blues not precise
smoked from sessions white with gin;

Born old, you could hear it in his laugh
jerking harsh and long after the joke,
and those huge hands demanding strings
for all the blues they'd had;

Finessing the battered Falcon
in a four-wheel spin up the track
beyond the creek bed to the commune shack
twice a year to see his kid.

And a fellow with neat clipped nails
thought his classical technique was better;
said, 'Hey! Let's do a gig at the pub!'
And stole the amp.

Cub nights

Mr Schlesinger and my father
took it week-about;
he would pull up and
wait in his solid old Hillman,
lights on, engine idling,
up on the street
as another uniformed boy
ran down a long brick pathway
to a lit front porch,
darkness closing snap!
like a barbed-wire memory.

From no place and to every destination…

From no place and to every destination
grey syllables to a harsh discordant sun,
blue moon and all the forties heartache
lived the journeying of harp and spoon;
Welsh seacoast and the swinging boats,
the whip of sand on bare legs, gardens made;
trains, ships, school uniforms, family snaps,
so many places' daylight out of rhyming time.
Small, home's a halt between old and new,
dirt caught under the fingernails when packing up;
No friends outlast the suitcase on the wharf,
the smell of grease slugs warming on the winches;
But eyes now carry a lighter footstep,
the past is put to bed each night with kisses;
The heart spells stories from no commonplace
to no place and every destination.

Diseases of the heart

The insurance doctor does a battery of tests;
the reasons they'll refuse to cough up
go on and on:
No family members died of syphilis or insanity?
no genetic abnormality?
no goitre nor constriction of the bowel?
He pokes and prods –
it might as well be Zanzibar –
roughly so many years of work left in you yet.
'And have you ever been diagnosed with
diseases of the heart?'
How should I answer that?
Some things don't show on X-rays
no less radical than your classic infarction;
What lifts or dashes hopes?
what makes the empty whole?
what gives the reason and fuel of being if not
diseases of the heart?

Fridge door

> For Kristina and Greg

Fridge door's white enamel canvas,
Dante made a flower from a ring of 'b's;

'Tim' and 'Jude' redone as rainbows;
'milk' – could be shopping list? spelling test?

Opening to white wine, breakfast coffee;
someone's left 'I l o v e y o u' all curled up;

Full magnetic jumble, days and nights;
Einstein was wrong: warmth is made with ice.

Life class

Eyes chase the discipline of light and shade:
charcoal, pencil, pastel, chalk or india ink,
all inclined to the wellhead of the mystery,
barely a ripple on the reservoir below, heater hissing;
One nipple trembling in the draught says Look!
This is not stone.

Friday night in Mandalay

Hot Friday evening lazy by the huge red fort,
mosquitoes slow from the moat, the sun slaps down;

Open shopfronts, women count a wedge of notes –
eccentric denominations fall into line;

After dark we drive past the old wooden cinema –
a queue all along the street and up the stairs;

Then thunder and the downpour brings the blackout –
English bikes, a Nissan, swerve to higher ground;

And at the blacked-out cinema the crowd's still waiting,
projectionist threading his old machine by touch –

And all along the same cracked muddy flagstones,
children play their timeless games by candlelight.

One starry night…

One starry night
three poets climbed into
a hot air balloon
and talked and talked and talked
and lifted off the ground.

On wings of their companionship
they rose and rose, drifting on
a gentle stream of consciousness
over field and forest, city and town

Till one stood up and said,
'Thanks, fellas, it's been most elevating',
stepped over the side
and walked off into the stars.

The basket swerved alarmingly
and suddenly realising
how clear the air, how bright the sky,
how close they were to heaven,
the other two were dumbstruck

and gently floated down.

Perspective

Little did they imagine its curative properties;
two dimensions were fine for the ancients
whose world had only three;
a revolution shattered the wisdom of flat space
and the slow architecting of heaven from colours
without time. How was one to live in structures
whose roofs fall away, converging to
the horizon before vanishing?

This new wave flattened
the curvature of light inside the eyeball,
froze the rotation of the head into a moment of blocks.
After the shock it became naïve to draft without it –
distortion rejected only by the wisdom of the blind.
And just as mathematicians grew a forest of proportions
this too failed to envisage the algebra of things
that become events when heated.

And sentiment defers to acceleration where life-objects
make distance and consume: we still don't have it –
how to capture love, longing, friendship, hope
with these dangerous probabilities?
The Sun trumpets realism with a childish eye;
grown-ups pledge elliptical courtships;
yet the mind's contentment weights things
for tomorrow, lighter than air.

Armistice in Brunswick Street

Red poppy redeeming not this anger,
plane trees clattering in the street
outgrew an overdose at the place next door –

A fly bashed through a leadlight pane
stopped the Warring States and a three-year-old
searched the bay-window looking-glass into this,

where the bath sighed quietly through the floorboards
and the old gas heater threatened asphyxiation.

And there, down Blythe Street,
she lived one long and almost carefree summer,
kisses pawned for the one sweet child and a text
growing three pages a day out of a typewriter –

We deceive with these exchanges;
the promise corrupts; the end never justifies;

tramstop strangers remind
we are ciphers in a plot we never see
and if we saw, would not remember.

So I bought one blood red poppy – a dollar –
for my two brave grandfathers
and for the flow of her lost tidal rivers,
still pondering reparation.

Sabina's violin

Sabina was a gypsy,
Sabina was wild;

she talked loudly and her mouth was big
and her hands would fly –

She had her father's violin;
ours were borrowed from the school.

Hers had nailmarks,
flaking varnish, grooves on the fingerboard;
ours were chestnut and ebony and smooth and new.

Ours had silver strings, hers had catgut;
ours said orchestra; hers said history.

She played it strongly –
She was dark and lonely.

We handed ours in at the end of the year.

She passed hers on.

This is the bed...

It stood, a humble four-legged maple thing
and the furniture man said:
This is the bed your father loved your mother in
This is the bed.
This is the bed that lived before time and the waters broke.
This is the bed where Van Gogh lay and bled –
bandage, pillowcase, mattress-ticking, head
all one single scab of red —
This is his bed.
This is the bed of Oscar Wilde or Juliette or Beatrice
or Cassanova or Adolf Hitler or Queen Victoria
or Frieda Lawrence or Lloyd George or Gertrude Stein
or Virginia Woolf or John and Yoko or you and me –
Which is your preferred bed?
This is the bed shoved the length of the High Street
curled in toilet paper and a girl in a bra
by the boys from Med
til its castors cracked in laughter on a gutter's edge —
This is that coming last hysterically funny bed.
This is the bed an old spinster gave as her
home address when names had gone and no one came
but a lady in white who called her 'Dear' and patted her head —
This is her vacant and afterwards so empty bed.
This is the bed Sally knelt on to slip the shirt
over her head close enough to catch her heaven scent —
This is that one and special bed.
This is the bed the hero died in shot through at Casino
and the coward later but no less certainly dead
after a bungled bullet through the head —
This is that last and mortal bed.

This is the bed of the man who turned to his wife and said;
'I love you' when he'd lost the right to
and where, after 'Sorry', she gently held his head —
This is that catholic and all-forgiving bed.
This is the bed of all hotels that all affairs have been in;
This is that joyfully crumpled and enseamèd bed.
This is the bed of incest and of poets dreaming
of all the courtesans of Venice, of sweat and love well-read.
This is the bed in Alexandra Hospital
where a Japanese soldier bayoneted —
This is a bowing-low now deeply sorry bed.
This is the birth bed of the mother in Gaza
where they laid a Koran in place of a whole body
when the boy was dead;
This is the bed in the ghetto where they hid the bread;
This is the bed of beds that is Jerusalem
where breath first moved on the face of the waters
and life was bled —
This is that first and incommunicable bed.
And one fine Tuesday morning Mr Ainger of Melbourne said;
'Your bid, I think, madam..?'
and the pretty lady in the hat was flustered,
looked down at her catalogue again and said,
'I'm sorry…'
and all in the dark varnish of that dust and sunlit morning,
went slightly red
and left it there instead.

The toymaker

Hands as calloused as the carpenter's and yet
you don't see them hefting rafters
high above the ground

Eye as true as the cabinetmaker's and yet
not tuned to the practicalities of
domestic joinery

Overalls as blue and crusted with shellac and
dried glue, workshop as airy, as piled
with sweet woodshavings

House as tidy, life as long,
bread as wholesome, beer as strong and yet

Something in the slope of his shoulders, in his
slow speech, in the way he looks at children
betrays an unquiet dreaming

Never made his peace with a big world
scaled one-to-one.

Song for Anna's third wedding

Like that first rendition of a Mozart piece
on a high stage all alone
in front of parents, teachers, classmates, friends
it doesn't matter that
the score fell from the music stand,
or the G-string unpegged itself towards E-flat,
or the mood or the pitch was wrong;
we clapped because you managed not to cry.

Life's a circus not a sonatina; it's
playing the fiddle and singing at the top of your voice
and tap dancing and pirouetting on a unicycle;
The only failure is failure of the heart.
And the trick I think is this: drink lots of lemonade,
wear shoes that grip;
leave out the notes you don't like;
lean forward boldly; and pedal like the devil.

Ode to an antique typewriter

Maybe you typed dispatches from Kokoda
or minutes for the church,
a thesis, an experimental play,
translations from the Tang
or hearty recipes;
Gutenberg without the trainer-wheels,
literature's flying shuttle;

You weighed a ton.
If I'd one day thrown you from the top step
the kids next door'd be still
picking bits out of their bike tyres.
Headline:
q w e r t y bites bitumen,
a humiliation of alliteration.

I couldn't fudge with you;
I couldn't swap a line or a stanza just for kicks;
it'd have to be all worked out again:
clean sheet into the roller, buzz it round,
thump thump thump
bash pigment through the soggy ribbon,
every character an act of will
bling!
Shove the bloody carriage back again.

And imagine if you could tell the tale
of all the stuff punched into you;
you *were* the twentieth century;
This plastic thing with all the latest graphics
doesn't get the images.

God, if the pen is mightier than the sword,
Oh Oliver, then you were mightier
than the cash register!

www.ingramcontent.com/pod-product-compliance
Lightning Source LLC
Chambersburg PA
CBHW062153100526
44589CB00014B/1813